Health Matters

Your Health

by Jillian Powell

an imprint of Hodder Children's Books

Titles in the series

Drugs and Your Health
Exercise and Your Health
Food and Your Health
Hygiene and Your Health

Editor: Sarah Doughty
Design: Sterling Associates
Illustrations: Jan Sterling
Cover design: Tony Fleetwood
Cover photograph: Tony Stone

First published in Great Britain in 1997 by
Wayland Publishers Ltd

This paperback edition published in 2002 by
Hodder Wayland, an imprint of Hodder Children's Books

Hodder Children's Books
A division of Hodder Headline Limited
338 Euston Road, London NW1 3BH

British Library Cataloguing in Publication Data
Powell, Jillian
Food and Your Health – (Health matters)
1. Nutrition – Juvenile literature
I. Title
612.3

ISBN 0 7502 4181 0

Printed in Hong Kong

Picture acknowledgements
Cephas 5, 13 both, 18; Chapel Studios 19, 25 top, 26;
Greg Evans 15, 23, 25 bottom; Impact 29 (Roger Scruton);
J. Allan Cash 7, 17, 24; Tony Stone 10 (Gray Mortimore),
12 (Steve Outram); Wayland Picture Library 4, 6, 9, 11, 14,
16, 20, 21, 22, 27, 28.

Contents

Food and your body

Your body is made up of the food you eat. You need lots of different kinds of food to stay healthy. We call this having a balanced diet. Everything you eat and drink is part of your diet.

Different foods contain different nutrients which help the body work properly. Protein is used to build and repair your body. Carbohydrates give you energy. Fats keep you warm and can be stored in the body for energy. Vitamins and minerals help keep you healthy.

Proteins are the body builders – bones, muscles, skin, hair and tissues.

Carbohydrates are a good source of energy.

Vitamin A is good for your eyes, bones and teeth.

Vitamin C keeps your bones and skin healthy and fights illness.

Iron keeps your blood healthy.

Calcium keeps your bones and teeth strong.

Fats help to keep you warm and can be kept in the body for energy.

These are the main types of foods you need.

FATS

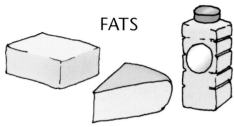

PROTEINS

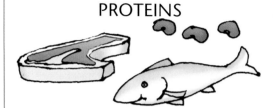

CARBOHYDRATES

VITAMINS & MINERALS

Eating a healthy diet helps to keep your body fit, and gives you lots of energy.

Cut out pictures of different types of food from newspapers and magazines. Stick them onto card to make a collage, dividing them into the different types of nutrients. Think about the food you eat in one meal. Which groups do these fall into?

Food and digestion

When you eat, your body breaks down the food so it can use the parts it needs. This is called digestion. First you bite into food and chew it with your teeth. The food mixes with saliva in your mouth which softens it and starts to break it down.

You swallow the food, and muscles push it down a long tube into your stomach where it mixes with juices which break it down. The mashed-up food moves into the small intestine and mixes with more juices. The nutrients then pass into the blood or go to the liver to be stored. Waste parts go into the large intestine where water is squeezed out. You get rid of the waste when you go to the toilet.

Left: Your body is about 66 per cent water.

Chewing is the first part of digestion. Food is softened by chewing and saliva.

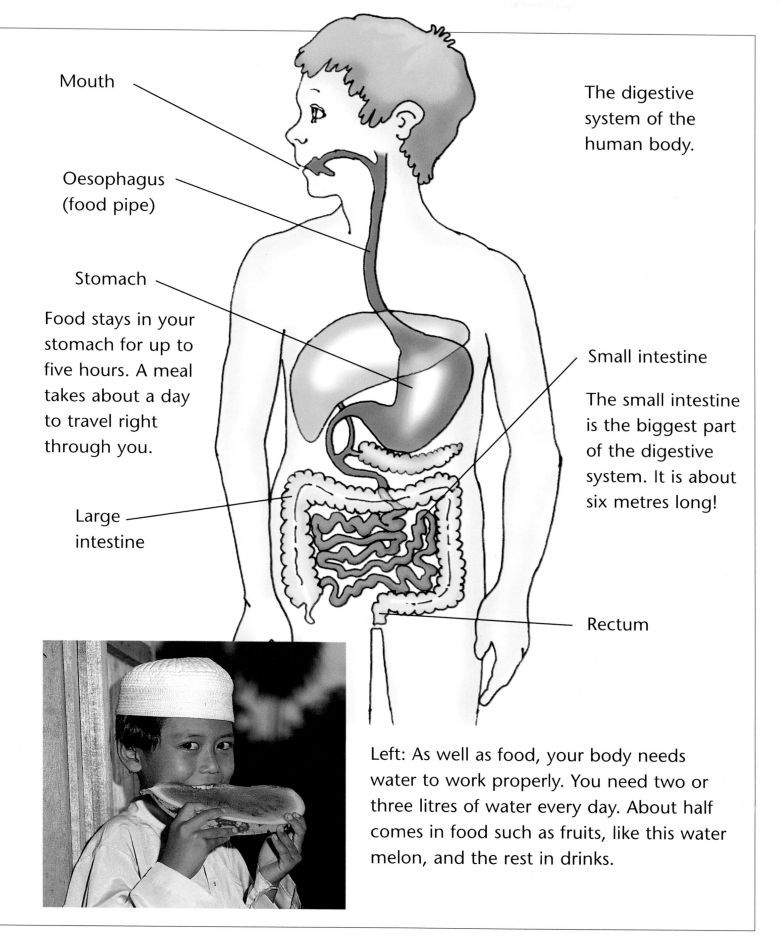

Mouth

Oesophagus
(food pipe)

Stomach

Food stays in your stomach for up to five hours. A meal takes about a day to travel right through you.

Large intestine

The digestive system of the human body.

Small intestine

The small intestine is the biggest part of the digestive system. It is about six metres long!

Rectum

Left: As well as food, your body needs water to work properly. You need two or three litres of water every day. About half comes in food such as fruits, like this water melon, and the rest in drinks.

Food for growing

Your body is made up of millions of tiny parts called cells. Until you are about 18 years old, your body makes new cells in order to grow. It also needs to repair and replace old cells all your life. The energy to make and repair body cells comes from your food. Body-building foods contain protein.

Your body is made up of cells, which are repaired and replaced throughout your life.

Bone cell

Nerve cell

Protein comes from animals and plants. Foods which contain lots of protein include meat, fish, eggs, cheese, milk, nuts and pulses. When you digest your food, proteins are broken down so they can be used to build different body parts like muscles, hair, skin and blood cells.

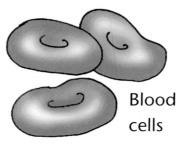
Blood cells

Muscle cells

Protein helps build muscle. There are about 650 muscles in your body. Almost half your weight is muscle!

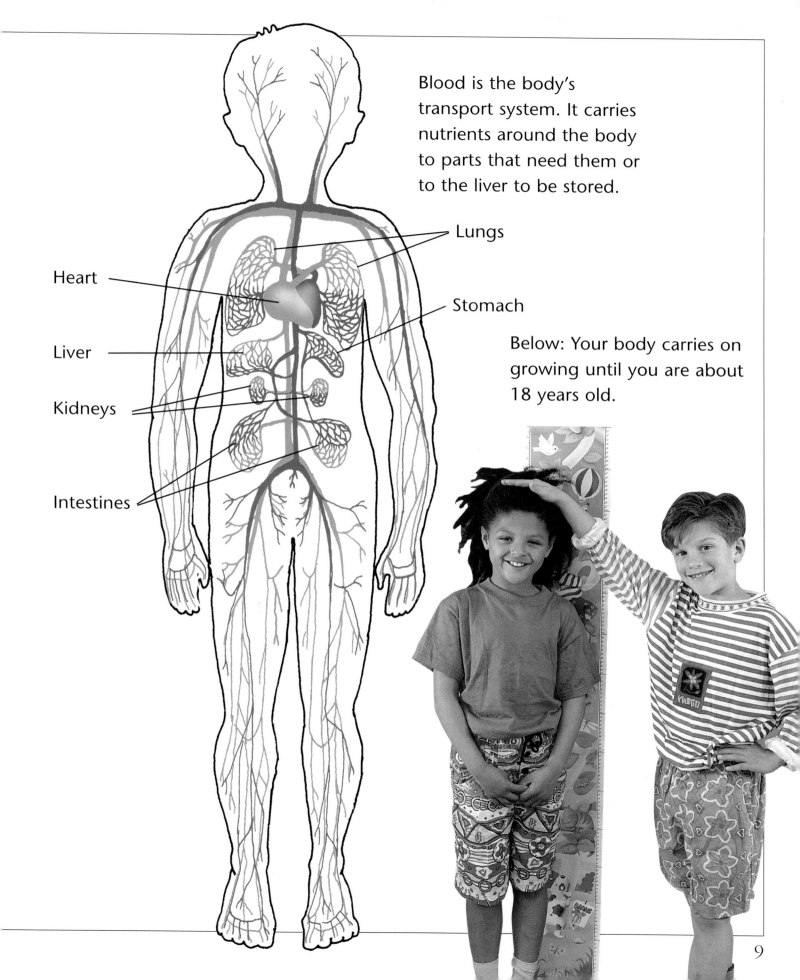

Blood is the body's transport system. It carries nutrients around the body to parts that need them or to the liver to be stored.

Lungs

Heart

Stomach

Liver

Below: Your body carries on growing until you are about 18 years old.

Kidneys

Intestines

Food for energy

Food gives your body energy. Your body needs energy to grow, repair itself and stay active.

Foods which give your body lots of energy are starchy carbohydrates like pasta, bread, cereals, rice and potatoes. They also contain some protein, vitamins and minerals. About a third of all the food you eat should be starchy carbohydrates. They should be the main part of each meal.

People who play sports eat lots of starchy foods to give them energy.

Energy in food and drink is measured in calories.

1 calorie = 1 kcal = 4.2 kjoules

(1 calorie is the amount of energy needed to raise the heat of 1 kg of water by one degree centigrade)

A glass of milk containing l00 calories will give you enough energy to dance for ten minutes, or watch television for $1\frac{1}{4}$ hours.

These foods contain 100 calories

| 50g bread | 100g bananas | 20g nuts | $1\frac{1}{2}$ apples |

Carbohydrates are found in foods like potatoes.

As children grow, they need approximately the following number of calories per day:

Boys
2,400 - 2,800

Girls
2, 200 - 2,400

Boys need more energy because they are generally bigger than girls.

Fats in food

You need some types of fat to keep you healthy but many people eat too much fat. Fatty foods can make you overweight and stop your heart working properly.

Some fats are easy to see, like fat on meat, fried foods and cream. Others are hidden in foods like cakes, biscuits, sausages, ice-cream and nuts. Fats keep the body warm and give you energy. The fat in oily fish like sardines and tuna can help the blood flow round the body, but the fats found in meat and dairy foods can make the blood too sticky and cause heart disease.

There are types of fats, called saturates, monounsaturates and polyunsaturates. For a healthy heart, cut back on saturates like animal fats.

Oily fish are a healthy source of unsaturated fats.

Types of fats

SATURATED
Milk
Cream
Butter
Coconut oil
Bacon

UNSATURATED
(poly and mono)
Olive oil
Sunflower oil
Grapeseed oil
Soya oil
Fish oil

Cutting down on fat

Jacket potatoes rather than chips

Fat per 100g		
	Jacket potatoes	0.2g
	Chips, fried	6.7g

Yoghurt rather than cream

Fat per 100g		
	Yoghurt, plain, low-fat	0.8g
	Cream, double	48.0g

Chicken rather than beef

Fat per 100g		
	Roast chicken, no skin	4.0g
	Roast beef	21.0g

Food which has been grilled, steamed or stirfried is less fatty than food fried or roasted in fat.

Sunflower oil comes from the seeds of the sunflower plant.

Make a list of what you eat each day, and discover how much fat is in your food. Look on labels of foods such as biscuits to see if they contain fats. Do you eat more saturated or unsaturated fats?

Food and body weight

You need to eat enough food to be the right weight for your height. If you eat more than you need, the extra food is stored as fat. If you don't eat enough food, your body can't grow or repair itself properly and you may get ill. It is not healthy to be too fat or too thin. If you are overweight, you need to cut down the number of calories in your food and drink and get more exercise.

Starchy foods like pasta and potatoes, and fresh fruit and vegetables contain lots of goodness but they are not fattening. Fatty and sugary foods like fried foods, cakes and biscuits contain more calories so they can make you put on weight.

Find out if you have a healthy weight for your height. It will change as you grow!

Left: Foods that are not converted to energy can turn to fat, which is stored under the skin all around the body.

Food rules

- Eat regular meals.
- Don't skip meals.
- Eat lots of starchy foods like bread and pasta.
- Eat plenty of fresh fruit and vegetables.

Right: Eating too many foods that are high in fats and sugar can make you overweight.

This pie chart shows you how much to eat of each of these types of foods:

- Bread, cereals and potatoes
- Meat, fish and alternatives
- Fat and sugar
- Milk and dairy products
- Fruit and vegetables

Fibre in food

Fibre is a part of food which cannot be digested. It passes through and helps push waste out of your body. After you have swallowed your food, it is squeezed along tubes inside you. You need to eat fibre to help the tubes squeeze properly.

Fibre comes from plant foods like cereals vegetables and fruits. We eat it in bread, pasta, rice, cereals, fruit and vegetables. The fibre in fruit and vegetables including peas and beans can help the blood flow round the body properly.

Foods with no fibre include:

cheese, sugar, fish, meat, ice-cream, eggs, oil, fruit drinks

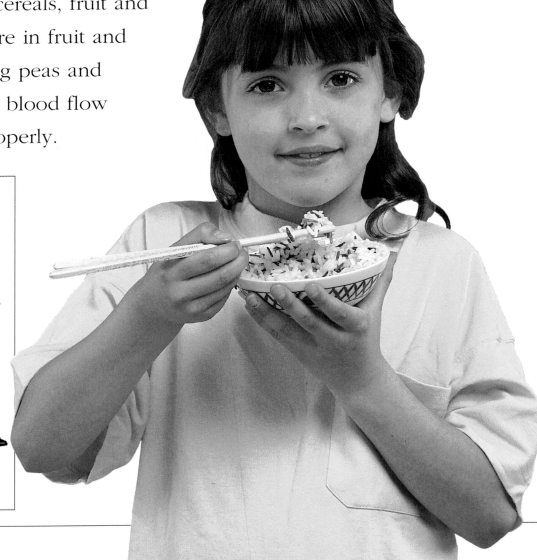

Foods like wild rice and wholegrain rice contain much more fibre than white rice.

High fibre foods (per 100g)

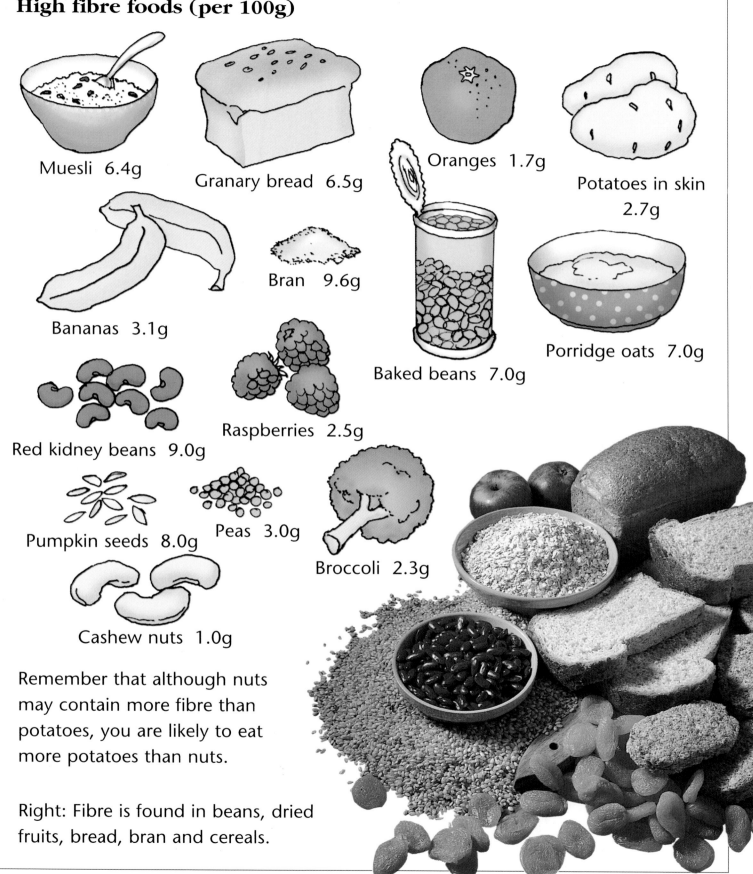

Muesli 6.4g

Granary bread 6.5g

Oranges 1.7g

Potatoes in skin
2.7g

Bananas 3.1g

Bran 9.6g

Baked beans 7.0g

Porridge oats 7.0g

Red kidney beans 9.0g

Raspberries 2.5g

Pumpkin seeds 8.0g

Peas 3.0g

Broccoli 2.3g

Cashew nuts 1.0g

Remember that although nuts
may contain more fibre than
potatoes, you are likely to eat
more potatoes than nuts.

Right: Fibre is found in beans, dried
fruits, bread, bran and cereals.

Vitamins and minerals

Eating lots of different foods gives you the vitamins and minerals you need to stay healthy. Vitamins and minerals all help different parts of the body.

Vitamin C helps keep teeth, gums and bones healthy and helps you fight colds. Vitamin K helps scars to heal. The mineral calcium makes strong teeth and bones and iron makes healthy red blood cells.

We only need tiny amounts of vitamins and minerals, but if we do not have enough, the body cannot work properly.

Fresh fruit and vegetables contain lots of vitamins and minerals. About a third of all the food you eat should be fruit and vegetables. Raw fruit and vegetables contain most vitamins.

Some important vitamins and minerals and foods they are found in.

Vitamin A
butter, eggs, carrots

Vitamin B1
cereals, milk, bread, meat, vegetables

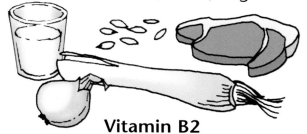

Vitamin B2
milk, cheese, eggs, meat, vegetables

Vitamin C
oranges, tomatoes, peppers

Vitamin D
oily fish, eggs, nuts, vegetables

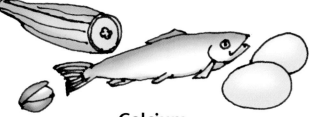

Calcium
milk, cheese, bread

Iron
sardines, beef, liver

A glass of milk is a good source of calcium. It also contains Vitamins A, B2 and D.

Salt is a mineral. We need about 3 grams of salt a day but most of us eat up to five times more! We add some salt to food but about two thirds comes in processed foods. Too much salt can lead to heart problems. Try not to add salt to food and cut down on salty foods like crisps and bacon.

Food and your teeth

Eating too many sweet foods can rot your teeth. Little scraps of food left in your mouth feed bacteria which grow in warmth and moisture. Sugar makes bacteria grow fastest. The sugar and bacteria cover your teeth with a sticky coat called plaque.

Eating crunchy foods like apples and carrots help keep your teeth clean and your gums healthy.

Plaque contains acids which can eat into the enamel on your teeth. If the acids make a hole, bacteria can get inside and rot the tooth so it will need a filling. Brushing your teeth after meals helps stop plaque forming.

The average person eats their own weight in sugar every year.

Sweets contain lots of sugar so always brush your teeth after eating sweets.

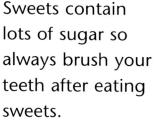

Tooth rules

- brush your teeth at least twice daily
- change your toothbrush every two months
- use dental floss to clean between your teeth
- see the dentist twice a year

You know when you add sugar to food but did you know that foods like cakes and biscuits, soups, sausages and baked beans all contain sugar? Look on food cans, jars and packets and make a list of all the foods that have sugar added. How much does each contain? Can you find any of the same sorts of food that have no added sugar?

Food additives

A lot of the food we buy today comes ready for us to cook or eat. Additives are chemicals which are added to make food last longer, taste better or look nicer.

Natural additives come from plants, like beetroot which gives a red colour. Others are made with chemicals, like saccharin which sweetens but has fewer calories than sugar. Preservatives help food last longer. Colourings add colour. Flavourings make flavours stronger.

There are also additives which make foods smoother and creamier. They stop fats and water from separating in foods like ice-cream and peanut butter.

Additives should be listed on the outside of all packaged foods.

Natural colourings from plants.

Beta carotene is orange and comes from carrots

and the colour red comes from beetroot.

These foods all contain additives:

Ham, bacon, sausages

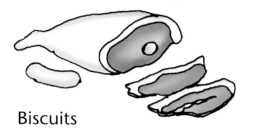

Pie fillings

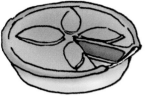

Packaged soups

Biscuits

Sandwich spread

Drinks

These sweets have had artificial colours added to them.

Compare labels of the same foods that contain additives. Look carefully at the packet to see what it contains compared with another brand.

Problem foods

Some people cannot eat certain foods because they make them ill. This is called having a food allergy.

Foods like milk, eggs, bananas, oranges and peanuts can make some people sick. Food additives can also make some people ill. Children can become hyperactive if they eat food colourings like Tartrazine and Sunset Yellow. People with diabetes must not eat too many sugary or sweet foods.

Some people cannot eat anything which contains wheat or wheat flour, such as cereals, bread, cakes or biscuits.

Some people cannot eat these foods as they are allergic to them:

prawns

mussels

nuts
strawberries

milk
eggs
bananas

People who have a wheat allergy cannot eat bread made from wheat flour.

Some people don't eat meat because of their religion. Hindus and some Sikhs don't eat meat. Muslims and Jewish people don't eat pork.

Religion and food

Hindus do not eat beef as a cow is considered a holy animal.

Buddhists respect all living creatures, as they believe they have a soul that will be reborn.

Sikhs do not eat beef, but it is not forbidden to do so.

Muslims have 'halal' (permitted) and 'haram' (not permitted) foods. They do not eat pork or its products as it is thought 'unclean'.

Jews have laws that state if food is clean or unclean. Sheep, cows and goats are clean, but the pig is 'unclean'.

Some religions also have rules about how food should be prepared.

Additives can give you:
Skin rashes
Stomach upsets
Breathing difficulties

Vegetarian food does not include meat. Vegetarians think it is wrong to kill animals for food and they don't like the way animals are farmed. Some people think it is healthier to eat a vegetarian diet.

Food safety

The food we eat must be fresh and clean or it can make us ill. Bacteria need warmth and moisture to grow so keeping food cold in a refrigerator or frozen can help it last longer. Bacteria from raw foods especially meat, can spread to cooked foods so they must be kept apart.

Foods like fruit and salads should be washed before we eat them to get rid of any germs and chemical sprays. Cooked foods, especially poultry and pork, must be cooked right through to kill any bacteria which could make us ill. If food has been frozen, it must be properly defrosted before it is cooked or it may not get cooked through.

Bacteria are tiny living things. Thousands could fit onto a pinhead. If we eat food which has bacteria on it, it can make us ill.

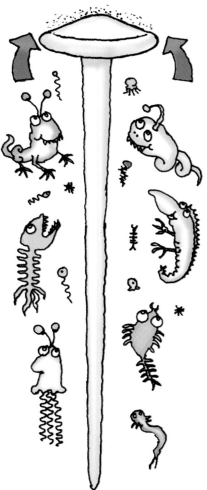

Left: Wash vegetables thoroughly as they may still contain chemicals.

Food goes bad when bacteria start growing on it. Bacteria can make bread go mouldy, milk and cream go sour and fruit juice go fizzy.

Food Safety Rules

- Always wash hands before touching food
- Keep everything in the kitchen clean
- Don't cough or sneeze over food
- Keep pets, flies and mice away from food

Collect labels from processed foods like yoghurts, cans, frozen and chilled meals. What are the storage instructions? Which last longest? Which last the shortest time? Make a chart showing how different types of food should be stored.

Healthy food

Having a healthy, balanced diet means eating lots of different foods which give your body the nutrients it needs. Health foods include natural foods like wholemeal bread and wholegrain rice, beans and lentils. They contain important nutrients like carbohydrates and vitamins but no added sugar, salt or additives. Organic food is food farmed without using chemicals.

Unhealthy foods are foods like sweets, lollies, cakes, biscuits and fizzy drinks. They contain lots of sugar, fat and additives and no important nutrients. It is best to eat them as treats now and again.

Ice-creams are eaten as treats now and again.

A *balanced diet*

There are five main food groups.

1. Starchy foods like cereals, potatoes, pasta, rice

3. Fruit and vegetables

2. Dairy foods like milk, butter, cheese

5. Fatty and sugary foods like cakes and biscuits

4. Meat, poultry and fish

A balanced meal contains food from each of the first four groups. Group five foods should only be eaten as treats now and again.

Some people prefer to buy food that has been produced at an organic farm.

When we talk about fast food we usually mean ready-to-eat foods like burgers, hot dogs and fries. An apple is healthy fast food because it comes ready to eat and it is good for you and your teeth. Design a poster selling an apple as healthy fast food.

Glossary

Bacteria Tiny living things. Some can be harmful but others are helpful.

Calories How we measure energy in food.

Carbohydrate A part of food which gives us energy.

Defrosted Letting something frozen warm up until no ice is left.

Diabetes A disease which means the body can't control the amount of sugar glucose in the blood.

Digestion What the body does to break food down and use nutrients.

Fat A part of food which keeps us warm and gives energy.

Food allergy When people cannot eat certain foods because they make them ill.

Hyperactive Over-energetic.

Nutrients Goodness in food which the body can use.

Protein A part of food which we need to grow and repair body cells.

Vegetarian Someone who does not eat meat.

Vitamins and Minerals Nutrients found in food which we need to keep us healthy.

Wholemeal and wholegrain Cereals which have the whole grain and have not had any part taken away.

Books to read

Body Maintenance Nicola Baxter (Health Education Authority, 1993)

Diet and Health Ida Weeks (Wayland, 1991)

Food and Digestion Steve Parker (Franklin Watts, 1989)

Healthy Food Anne Qualter and John Quinn (Wayland, 1993)

The Stomach and Digestive System Carol Ballard (Wayland, 1996)

What's Inside Us? Anita Ganeri (Macdonald Young Books, 1994)

You and Your Food Judy Tatchell and Dilys Wells (Usborne, 1991)

For leaflets about food

Food Sense
London SE99 7TT

The Distribution Department
HEA (Health Education Authority)
Hamilton House
Mabledon Place
London WC1H 9TX

Index